The Little Book of
LIVING GREEN

by Mark Hegarty

Illustrations by Neil Bennett

Cover by Jim Lefevre

Nightingale

An imprint of Wimbledon Publishing Company
LONDON

Copyright © 2000
Illustrations © 2000 WPC

First published in Great Britain in 2000
by Wimbledon Publishing Company Ltd
P.O. Box 9779 London SW19 7ZG
All rights reserved

First published 2000 in Great Britain

ISBN: 1903222 13 3

Produced in Great Britain
Printed and bound in Hungary

Many thanks to all those people and organisations who kindly contributed their time and ideas to this book.

M.H.

The aim of this little book is to give you the information that will allow you to make a difference to the world around you. Most people are conscious of the facts surrounding the environment only as vague concepts, with little connection to their day-to-day lives. This book doesn't aim to reproach you for enjoying things that you have earned and deserved. It simply provides a few suggestions for 'low-maintenance' ways to limit the damage you might cause to the environment.

It really is easy to take environmental issues on board and it doesn't have to be a major commitment. By adopting just a few of these suggestions not only will you feel better, but you will add a little more weight to a growing tide of environmental responsibility, the cumulative effect of which will be huge.

Recycling

As recycling becomes increasingly important, local authorities are beginning to provide more and more recycling points. The variety of recyclable material is also growing fast. Plastics, wood, paper, tyres, glass, tins and cans, even clothes and shoes can all be recycled. In fact, all of Levi Strauss' new stationery is made from recycled denim off-cuts.

Giving to Charity

When you or your family grow out of
old clothes/books/furniture/boyfriends
take them to the charity shop.

What can and can't be recycled?

The recycling logo consists of three arrows forming a circle. It's known as a 'mobius loop'.

If the logo is displayed on a dark background ♻, it means the product or packaging is made from recycled material. If it's on a light background ♻, the material can be recycled.

Film and foil

Research has shown that, as well as helping the environment, re-useable containers will be more beneficial to your health than miles of aluminium foil or clingfilm. No doubt it will also reduce stress levels, by avoiding that infuriating moment when the foil or film runs out just too soon to cover what you're doing…

Rechargeable batteries

Using rechargeable batteries
saves a lot of energy, toxic chemicals
and money. (Although beware of
rechargeable batteries containing
cadmium: these are considered
environmentally harmful).

Disposable materials

Using polystyrene and plastic plates
and cups does untold damage to the
environment, and they take about 500
years to degrade. Wood-based
products such as paper cups cause
deforestation. Solution: drink from a
proper glass or a mug instead.
Everything tastes so much better, and
there is no temptation to nibble your
glass when you've finished your drink.

Lower taxes

Recycling can even lower your taxes: as well as reducing the amount of primary materials consumed (such as trees), recycling also reduces the amount of rubbish that occupies expensive landfill sites. And where do you think the council raises the money to pay for these sites?

Green bin men

Recycling doesn't have to involve any major hassle or commitment: almost everywhere, dustmen will pick up special bags for paper and/or other recyclable material from your doorstep, to be separated and recycled later. Phone your local authority and see what sort of scheme they run.

Recycling in the office

Most offices generate huge quantities of high quality paper waste. By establishing a recyclable paper bin, and simply using both sides of a piece of paper, you can make a difference both in terms of reducing office costs, and slowing deforestation. Each ton of recycled office paper saves 17 trees and 380 gallons of oil. Most councils will also charge lower business rates if you put your waste paper in a separate bag for collection and recycling.

Single use products are the spawn of
the devil and intrinsically evil...

Office savings

By recycling used cartridges/toners
from printers and photocopiers
through the manufacturers you can
make substantial savings for your
office, which should then be spent on
chocolate biscuits.
Winners all round.

What does recycled mean?

Buy recycled paper, but be aware that 'recycled' can mean a wide variety of things: some manufacturers who display the recycled logo include only small amounts of 'first hand' paper off-cuts rather than more eco-friendly 'post-consumer waste'. Using these off-cuts is of course better than wasting them, but is not the most environmentally friendly way to make paper products.

Eco-friendly paper

The most environmentally friendly
paper products are made from
sustainable forests (trees specifically
planted in managed woodland for
harvesting), tree-free paper (paper
made from other materials such as
hemp and straw), or contain a high
percentage of 'post-consumer waste'
(paper which has been used and
then recycled).

Newpaper

Big advances have been made in the recycling of paper: recycled paper goods are no longer the coarse, harsh or low quality products they once were. Recycled toilet paper, for example, is now just as soft as other varieties.

Composting household waste

As well as extending the all-too-brief lifespan of a bin bag, composting will also give you high quality fertiliser that avoids the financial and environmental cost of the chemical alternative. (NB: This one is best limited to those with gardens, unless you find the idea of a huge pile of rotting vegetables in your kitchen appealing.)

Standby

Remember to turn off lights and appliances when not in use. Even keeping appliances like your TV on standby still uses up electricity.

Eco-computing

Computers, despite their appetite for eating crucial files or crashing at critical moments, have streamlined many aspects of modern life and business. The 'paperless office' can make great environmental and economic savings by using emails and computer files rather than print-outs, folders etc.

Insulating windows and roofs

Well-fitted windows, an insulated roof, and double-glazing will make a big difference to your electricity bill, and also make your house quieter. Environmentally sound windows alone have been shown to pay for themselves on average three times over, while an insulated roof saves around £70 every year.

Microwaves

Microwaves use much less energy to heat food than ovens or stoves. They also heat water much faster and more efficiently than a kettle. Just remember not to leave the spoon in your coffee mug as you heat it.

Kettles

If you do use the kettle, try not to use
more water than you need. Heating
the extra water uses a lot of energy.
And it takes ages.

Green electricity

Since 1998, it has been possible to choose which company supplies your electricity. This gives you the opportunity to select a greener company who can provide you with electricity at a lower environmental cost. Check out Friends of the Earth's website (www.foe.org) for a breakdown of the performance of the different electric companies.

Washing machines
and dishwashers

Don't use washing
machines/dishwashers when they are
only half full. These appliances are
very expensive in terms of electricity
and water consumption, so making
sure you use them to maximum
efficiency will reap rewards. A typical
washing machine uses 95 litres of
water per wash, while two half loads
will use considerably more.

Keep a lid on it

When cooking on a hob, a huge
amount of energy can be lost through
evaporation. This loss of energy
(and time) can be largely eliminated
by making sure that you keep
well-fitting lids on pots and pans. It
also stops your kitchen from getting
steamed up, which can cause long-
term problems of damp and mould.

Light bulbs

Of the electricity used by normal
light bulbs, in most cases only 10%
of the energy is converted into light,
while the other 90% is turned into
heat. The electricity used just to
light a building is often as much as
50% of the total energy bill.

Bright idea

There are new and better versions of compact fluorescent bulbs available which use 25% less energy, and they last ten times as long as a traditional bulb. The savings over the lifetime of the bulb total £126.

Car fitness

Retuning your engine every 5,000 miles or so will make your car much more efficient. Just keeping your tyres inflated to the correct level has been shown to cut up to 10% of petrol costs. A healthier car also means you're less likely to get stranded in a lay-by with a flat tyre or smoke pouring out of your bonnet.

Smog

Half of all smog-producing emissions
could be saved if all cars were well
tuned.

A breath of fresh air

Walking to school or work is really good for all aspects of your health (and your waistline). But then, you knew that anyway... And as for pollution, recent experiments have proved definitively that pollution levels experienced by a pedestrian on the pavement are significantly lower than they are inside a car.

Bus it

Take the bus. I dare you. One busload
of people who would normally drive
means 40 cars off the road,
70,000 litres of fuel and 9 tonnes of
air pollution saved each year. It saves
the driver cash on petrol, repairs,
parking, road tax and insurance.

Easy rider

When driving, avoid braking too hard
and accelerating too quickly, and you
can reduce your petrol consumption
by up to 25% (as well as giving your
passengers a smoother ride).

Short trips

A high percentage of car journeys cover only very short distances. Cars are much less efficient, using more petrol and polluting more, when they're cold (i.e. at the start of journeys), on short journeys, and when in traffic.

Junk mail

Stop junk mail. Unless you're really really lonely, and need some post. Addresses are generally sold by credit card companies, so phone them to let them know you don't want them to sell your details. After all they do belong to you.

Hardwoods

If you are buying wood products, it is
best to avoid tropical hardwoods such
as Mahogany, Brazilian Cherry etc.
These products are very rarely farmed
in a sustainable way (i.e. trees that
have been planted specifically for
harvesting), and on average, 60 trees
will be felled to reach each
mahogany tree.

Smokeless fuel

Despite being fairly difficult to check up on, non-smokeless fuel is illegal in most urban environments.

No butts

Cigarette butts should be properly
disposed of in bins or ashtrays: you
can't always rely on a wandering
tramp to come and pick up the butts
you discard on the ground, and they
take an extremely long time to
decompose. Unless you smoke
roll-ups, of course. In which case you
probably are a wandering tramp.

Plant a tree

Plant a tree – to commemorate a new year, a birthday, an anniversary, your dead goldfish... just plant one! Or call the Woodland Trust who will plant (and dedicate) one for you in your area. It will even give you something solid to chain yourself to later on when they try to make space for a new by-pass.

Noise pollution

Noise pollution is a greatly under-estimated form of environmental damage that can put huge psychological pressure on the local wildlife. Yet another good reason to avoid heavy metal music…

Eco-tourism

Tourism is an industry that is growing fast on a global scale. While potentially a very positive phenomenon, tourism can also have a very negative effect on the environment. It is important to be aware of the effect of your trip on certain delicate ecosystems (e.g. coral reefs), and to make sure that you and your tour operators try to avoid any damage being caused by your trip.

Live forever?

According to a study by the Rand Corporation in the USA, every mile walked by a sedentary person adds an extra 21 minutes to their life. Which means that as long as you keep walking at 3 mph or more you will live forever...
Maybe.

Reviving dead lighters

While disposable lighters are not very
environmentally friendly, at least
there are ways of getting maximum use
out of them even after they run out of
fuel: while the empty lighter still
sparks you can use it to light the gas
on your hob or grill. That way you
won't need endless boxes of matches.

Showers vs Baths

Showers use about a third as much
water (and electricity) as baths.
A five minute shower every day rather
than a bath will save 400 litres of
water every week.

Share your bath

If you insist on having a bath, leave
the water for someone else in your
household to use. Or better still invite
a willing partner to share your bath.
Environmental altruism is a
great chat-up line.

Waterhog

30% of water consumed in the home is flushed down the toilet. You can reduce the amount of water used in each flush by fitting special 'lo-flow' devices, or by contacting your water company for a free 'hippo' or 'hog'. These displacement devices are very simple to install or remove, and save 3 litres per flush.

Have you got the bottle?

Alternatively, you can simply put a water-filled plastic bottle in the cistern, which will also decrease the amount of water used in each flush. (And you can easily increase the flow again by removing the bottle or 'hippo' should you need the extra flushing power…).

Dry Cleaning

Don't leave water running while shaving, cleaning teeth, washing dishes. Leaving a bathroom tap running will waste almost 9 litres per minute.

Aerosols

Don't use aerosols that contain CFCs.
Please note that this does not mean
deodorant should be foregone
altogether.

Chloro-Fluoro-Carbons

CFCs are also present in older fridges and car air conditioning units. The CFCs should be drained or recycled rather than allowing them to escape into the atmosphere when finished with. One CFC particle will destroy on average 100,000 of the ozone particles which protect the earth from the more damaging rays from the sun.

Speak through your wallet

A wide variety of products from coffee to bank accounts to shampoo are available from companies who do make environmental and ethical issues a major consideration. If you disagree with a company's ethical policy, then you can force them to change: don't buy their products.

Make yourself heard

The weight of public pressure, will eventually make unethical corporations change their policies. Texaco, Mitsubishi, Nike, Shell, Nestlé, Exxon, McDonalds etc. are all being targeted by campaigns to try to make them take green issues into greater account. If you invest in stocks and shares, you can ask your broker to avoid all companies that ignore ethical or environmental issues.

Endangered species

Don't buy anything in coral, ivory,
skins, pelts, tortoise shell etc.
Or shocking pink. Even in the
eighties, it never looked good.

Join up today

Join an environmental organisation
like WWF/Greenpeace/Friends of the
Earth/Rainforest Action Network: a
small annual payment makes very little
impact on your bank balance, but gives
important support to these organisations and lets you feel good all year
round. You can find out more from
their websites at these addresses:

www.wwf.org

www.greenpeace.org

www.foe.org

www.ran.org

Death by six-pack

Always cut up six-pack holders: if
they get into water supplies, they will
strangle birds that get tangled up in
them. They can also get stuck on
dolphins' noses, condemning them to a
slow death by starvation.

Unintended victims

100,000 dolphins die in fishing nets
every year. Many shops stock special
'dolphin--friendly tuna', caught using
nets that limit harm to dolphins.

Rags vs paper towels

Re-useable rags and cloths are a
better option than paper towels when
cleaning up spillages.

Re-using bags

Try to remember to take bags with you to the supermarket. Many supermarkets offer durable 'bags for life', which last considerably longer than the usual bags (and allow you to get bottles and tins home without the bag handles stretching and breaking).

'Guano Chic'

Don't waste your precious summer weekends washing your car: let the splattered droppings of the neighbourhood birds become an 'interesting new look', and save more than your weight in water.

Gardens

Pesticides and chemicals, whether in
the garden or on an industrial level,
are like prescription drugs:
undoubtedly they can have beneficial
effects, but the real issue is whether or
not the benefits of these chemicals
outweigh the inevitable side effects.
Often there are perfectly adequate
natural remedies which are cheaper,
less harsh on your garden, and which
use products already in your home (so
no extra hassle, cost, or packaging).

Complementary gardening

You can also take advantage of plants'
natural characteristics to the benefit
of your garden: by planting the right
plants you can attract the 'good'
insects (such as ladybirds etc.), and
repel the 'bad' ones (aphids, for
example). Find out more from a good
book on the subject.

Slugs and snails

Slugs and snails, being sensitive souls, find climbing over a bristly rope (or alternatively a border of shells or fine gravel) impossible because it tickles their sensitive undersides. And a rope around your herbaceous border won't make your cat sick on the kitchen floor like some chemical repellents.

Moles

Putting garlic cloves in molehills
understandably persuades
moles to move on.

Ants

To get rid of ants, sprinkle red pepper
or coffee grounds on the anthills.

Mosquitoes

Citronella, basil, anise oil, balsamic vinegar and fresh garlic are all effective mosquito repellents, and less harsh on your skin than conventional repellents. Of course, fresh garlic will naturally repel more than just mosquitoes…

Aphids

Spraying a little soapy water on your
plants will get rid of any aphid
problems, and won't create a potential
chemical hazard for wildlife,
pets or children.

Walk on the wild side

If you leave a part of your garden to become overgrown and wild, it will provide an area of refuge for local wildlife. And a good excuse to leave the lawn for a bit longer .

Personal reservoir

Keeping a barrel in your garden will collect rain for watering your plants, allowing you to reduce the amount of tap water used (and get through hosepipe bans with a verdant lawn).

DIY veggies

Grow some of your own vegetables and
herbs. Gardening is healthy, fun and
helps relieve stress. (It also impresses
dinner guests when you nonchalantly
mention that "basil picked fresh from
the plant tastes so much better…")

Easy life

Putting nuts out in winter make
easier for birds, and definite
brightens up cold winter mornin

URBAN
FOX
REFUGE

Hungry toads

There are effective and longer-term
natural solutions to many garden
infestations: for example, a toad
(available for £2 - 3 from a good pet
shop) will eat on average 1500 earwigs
over the course of a single summer.

Cleaning windows

White vinegar and water mixed together in equal measures make a great mirror and window cleaner, and zold newspaper will leave far fewer smears and smudges than rags or kitchen roll.

Scouring

For scouring bathroom surfaces, you
can simply use baking soda rather
than chemical cleaners.

Stain removers

Rather than buying a variety of different 'stain devils', you can use a quarter of a cup of borax in 2 cups of water to get rid of almost any stain.

Limescale

Boiling a cup or two of vinegar in your kettle will get rid of any limescale just as efficiently as more expensive chemical treatments. Just don't forget to empty and rinse it before you make tea.

Organic food

Organic food may be a little more expensive. It has to be really, but there are major benefits. On a personal level, food that has been grown without the support of a cocktail of chemicals will avoid all kinds of health hazards for the consumer. And on a larger scale, organic food doesn't wreak havoc on the environment.

Fresh fruit and veg

The fruit and vegetables you buy loose
are actually better for you than the
equivalent food in pre-packed form.
They are generally cheaper, and save
some of the huge volume of plastic
packaging we throw away every year.

Pesticides

Pesticide ingredients have been shown to cause, amongst other things, birth defects, cancer, and gene mutations. Scientists have speculated that the huge rises in various allergies, and even cancers, are due to the high levels of chemicals we are exposed to.

Rainforest burgers

Only one tenth of the food that animals eat is converted into meat. Some fast food restaurants have a reputation for using rainforest beef, and each individual burger farmed this way causes deforestation of an area the size of a kitchen.

Eat less meat

Scientists generally agree that eating less meat would significantly improve the health of most people in the developed world, as well as being more environmentally friendly. Consumption of large amounts of red meat in particular has been linked to heart problems. Besides which, meat is expensive.

Genetically modified food

This is a contentious issue about which
very few facts are really known.
Sounds like a good enough reason to
avoid it…

Fresh food

Eat as much fresh, local seasonal produce as you can. Food shipped halfway across the globe cannot be as fresh, and the levels of vitamins and nutrients decrease steadily once the food has been picked. Locally grown cauliflowers have the added advantage of not coming from land that was previously virgin rainforest.

There has been much research about the extent of environmental damage caused by industry and individuals.

The figures show that major damage has already been done, and we need to bring about a profound change in general behaviour.

The longer current destructive attitudes continue, the harder it will be to undo the damage.

The following pages contain some facts and figures that highlight why it is so crucial that we all do what we can to keep environmental damage to a minimum.

Jungle remedies

A quarter of all drugs in the chemists come from tropical forests. It is a fair assumption that there might well be cures for all sorts of incurable diseases (cancer, AIDS etc) nestling among the unknown plants and animals in the world's rainforests.

Going, going...

Over half of the world's tropical forest
has already been destroyed.

The progress of science

Since modern science began, we have catalogued less than 20% of all species on the planet. It has been calculated that the same percentage of species will become extinct over the next 20–40 years.

Cars and cars and cars

Half of all developed land in the US
is dedicated to cars.

Oil extraction

"Before Texaco came to Ecuador, our rivers, lakes, and streams had many fish, our waters were clean, and there was ample game in the forest. Now, our rivers are contaminated, the fish have disappeared, and the animals have gone away."

Arceliano Illanez, FCUNAE (organisation for Amazonian indigenous communities)

Think about it next time you drive round the corner to the video store.

Third world debt

Many third world countries are
crippled by debt caused by massive
loans and it is often the countries'
natural resources or social
programmes that pay the price.
Support banks such as the
Co-operative Bank, which is
campaigning to have third world debt
written off, and has pledged never to
invest money in unethical projects.

Sex change

As part of their seasonal lives, oysters
naturally change sex with a frequency
most of us would find quite traumatic.
Rising pollution levels in many rivers,
lakes and seas are causing the poor
oysters major problems in this
process. This in turn results in a large
number of same-sex oysters, and
inevitably problems of reproduction.

Downward spiral

Oysters are important natural filters and cleaners of water, and the falling number of oysters is causing a cycle of ever-increasing pollution problems in several major bodies of water (not to mention the local restaurants).
In polluting our waterways, we are often also destroying the rivers' and lakes' ability to revive themselves.

Rising temperatures

The 1990s was globally the hottest
decade ever recorded. Higher
temperatures will lead to diseases
spreading much faster and further.
The first malarial mosquito has
already been found on British shores.

Greenhouse effect

The 'greenhouse effect' has been happening naturally for a very long time, but only to a limited degree. Without it, the Earth's average temperature would be about $-18°C$, rather than the current $15°C$. Now that our pollution is hugely magnifying the greenhouse effect, temperatures are rising fast. Some regions are expected to experience temperature increases of more than $10°C$ over the next century.

World population

It has been calculated that the world can support 2 billion people at Western standards of living. The current world population is around 6 billion. Predictions show that in about 2050, within the lifetime (hopefully!) of much of the current population, the Earth's population will top 12 billion.

Galapagos tortoises

Some of the giant Galapagos tortoises
that inspired Charles Darwin's ideas
about evolution may well still be alive.
They can live for over two hundred
years, but sadly the effects of tourism
and settlers on the islands have lead
to the tortoises becoming an
endangered species.

Go forth and multiply.
A bit.

At the turn of the twentieth century, the world population was increasing by about 6 million per year. In the 1950s, that rate reached 18 million per year. Our current rate of increase is in excess of 100 million people per year. Make sure you don't add to the problem of overpopulation: try to keep *exactly* to the Western world's average of 2.4 children.

It's getting crowded...

10% of all humans that have lived
ever ever *ever* are alive today.

Slow progress

An American inventor by the spectacular name of Buckminster Fuller built a new car that will fly once technology makes the materials and engines available. On the road, the car can cover 30 miles on a gallon of petrol, and carry 11 passengers reaching speeds of 120 mph. Significantly more efficient than cars currently available, Fuller's 'Dymaxion car' was built back in 1933.

Exhaust

An average car emits two and a half
times its weight in carbon dioxide
each year.

Making a difference to the world around you doesn't have to be a titanic struggle, nor does it mean you have to commit yourself to anything demanding.

It is really just a question of respecting the world around you, and acting accordingly.

Personal reservoir

Keeping a barrel in your garden will
collect rain for watering your plants,
allowing you to reduce the amount of
tap water used (and get through
hosepipe bans with a verdant lawn).

DIY veggies

Grow some of your own vegetables and herbs. Gardening is healthy, fun and helps relieve stress. (It also impresses dinner guests when you nonchalantly mention that "basil picked fresh from the plant tastes so much better…")

Easy life

Putting nuts out in winter makes life
easier for birds, and definitely
brightens up cold winter mornings.

Walk on the wild side

If you leave a part of your garden to
become overgrown and wild, it will
provide an area of refuge for local
wildlife. And a good excuse to leave
the lawn for a bit longer .